D0402909

TO:

FROM:

212° THE EXTRA DEGREE

EXTRAORDINARY RESULTS BEGIN
WITH ONE SMALL CHANGE

SAM PARKER AND MAC ANDERSON

simple truths®
▸ Small books. BIG IMPACT.

IGNITE READS
spark impact in just one hour

Photo Credits
Internals: page vii, © Jose A. Bernat Bacete/Getty Images; page x, © aapsky/Shutterstock; page xii, by Freestockcenter/Freepik.com; page 4, © HQuality/Shutterstock; page 7, by Annie Spratt/Unsplash; page 8, © Dudarev Mikhail/Shutterstock; page 10, © Paul Bradbury/Getty Images; page 12, © Pavel1964/Shutterstock; page 18, by Andy Watkins/Unsplash; page 20, by Samantha Sophia/Unsplash; page 25, by Simson Petrol/Unsplash; page 26, by Josh Calabrese/Unsplash; page 28, by Markos Mant/Unsplash; page 30, © Digital Storm/Shutterstock; page 34, © Unuchko Veronika/Shutterstock; page 36, © BalkansCat/Shutterstock; page 38, by Anvesh Uppunuthula/Unsplash; page 40, © Emelianova Marina/Shutterstock; page 44, © Iurii Osadchi/Shutterstock; page 45, © BrunoRosa/Shutterstock; page 46, © MivPiv/iStock; page 49, © Amd Ly/EyeEm/Getty Images; page 50, by Lindsey Middleton/Unsplash; page 52, © ROBYN BECK/Staff/Getty Images; page 54, by William Stitt/Unsplash; page 56, © KTSDESIGN/SCIENCE PHOTO LIBRARY/Getty Images; page 58, by Brad Neathery/Unsplash; page 60, by Benjamin Ashton/Unsplash; page 62, by Pablo Heimplatz/Unsplash; page 65, by Nathan Dumlao/Unsplash; page 66, by Wayan Parmana/Unsplash; page 68, © Triff/Shutterstock; page 70, © Graham Finlayson/Contributor/Getty Images; page 72, by Robert Baker/Unsplash; page 74, Underwood & Underwood/Library of Congress/public domain; page 76, Underwood & Underwood/Library of Congress/public domain; page 80, Jon Tyson/Unsplash; page 83, by Greg Raines/Unsplash; page 84, by Thiago Cerqueira/Unsplash; page 87, by Christopher Burns/Unsplash; page 88, by Hanny Naibaho/Unsplash; page 91, © Monkey Business Images/Shutterstock; page 92, by Brad Neathery/Unsplash; page 95, by Alex Radelich/Unsplash; page 96, by Neonbrand/Unsplash; page 98, by Clique Images/Unsplash; page 100, by Orlova Maria/Unsplash; page 102, by Fab Lentz/Unsplash; page 105, by Patrick Tomasso/Unsplash; page 106, by Dan Bo/Unsplash; page 107, by Rob Bye/Unsplash; page 110, © Vaclav P3k/Shutterstock; page 113, by Ales Krivec/Unsplash

Published by Simple Truths, an imprint of Sourcebooks, Inc.
P.O. Box 4410, Naperville, Illinois 60567-4410
(630) 961-3900 • Fax: (630) 961-2168 • sourcebooks.com

Printed and bound in China.
OGP 10 9 8 7 6

FOR EVERYONE.

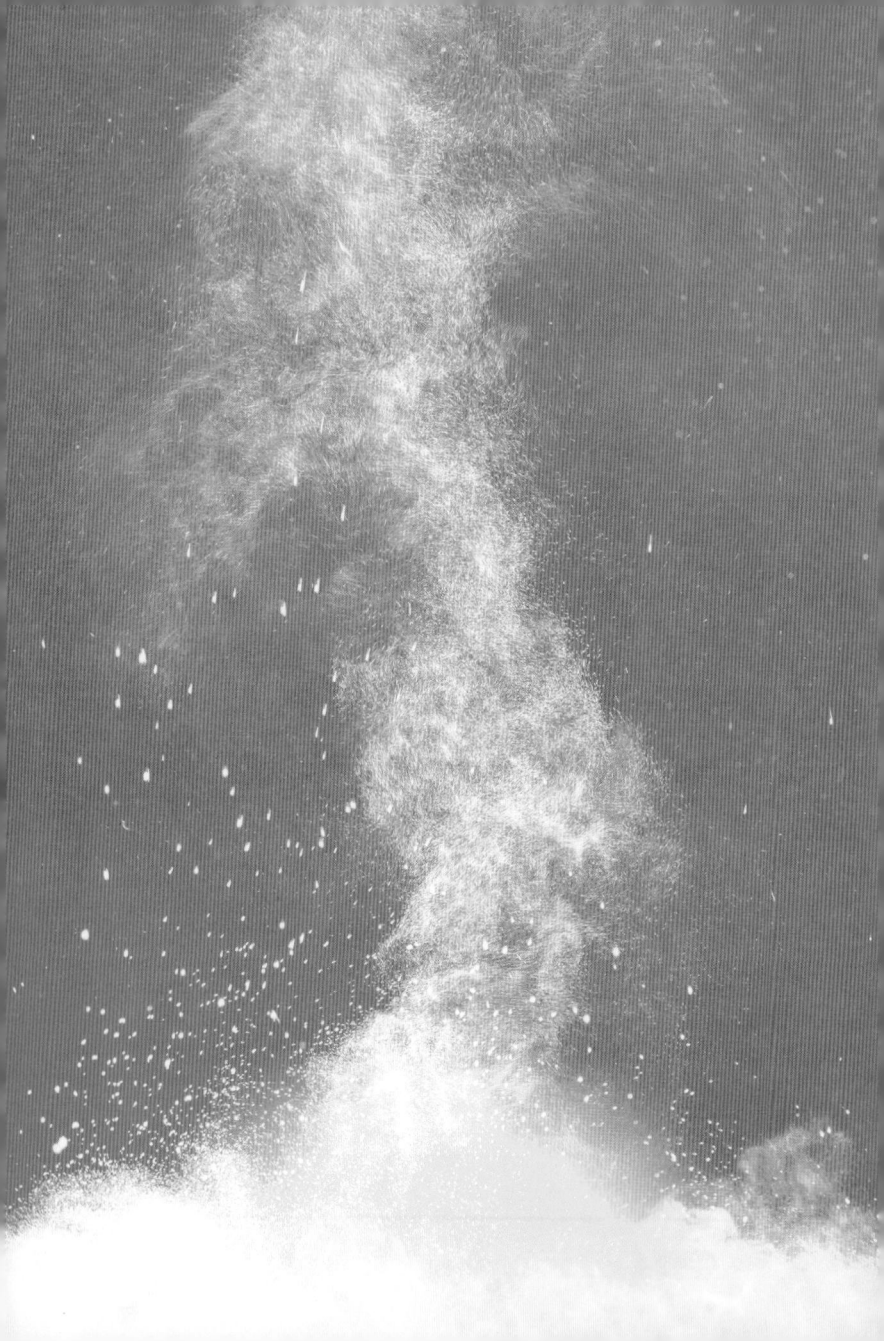

CONTENTS

At 211°, water is hot.
At 212°, it boils.
And with boiling water comes steam…
And with steam, you can power a **locomotive**.

ONE DEGREE

Raising the temperature of water by **one extra degree** means the difference between something that is simply very hot and something that generates enough force to power a machine—a beautiful, uncomplicated metaphor that ideally should feed our every endeavor— consistently pushing us to make the **extra effort** in every task we undertake. 212° serves as a forceful drill sergeant with its motivating and focused message, while adhering to a scientific law—a natural law.

It reminds us that seemingly small things can make tremendous differences. So **simple** is the analogy that you can stop reading right now, walk away with the opening thought firmly planted in your mind, and benefit from it for the rest of your life.

That's the purpose of this book—to help you internally define and take ownership of the most fundamental principle behind achieving life results beyond your expectations. This simple idea has a singular focus—an actionable focus.

212°

It's this dramatic—three numbers joined together to form one, crystallizing a message that absolutely assures life-altering, positive results for those who choose to apply it.

Still looking for the "silver bullet" or "quick fix" to achieving great results?

STOP.

Reams of material are written and taught with an approach to reaching an end by close-to-effortless means—and more will be written. Advertising messages continually promote methods for achieving end results with little or no effort. And this material and these messages are so effective that in many cases people will work harder to avoid the extra effort than to actually apply the effort that will produce the originally desired outcome.

Great materials with solid approaches to results have also been created and taught. Unfortunately, in so many cases, action on the part of the reader is the missing ingredient. And for those individuals who do take action, there is even a smaller number who make the extra effort necessary to reach the desired results. Books are purchased, programs are attended, and clubs are joined with wonderful intentions of putting forth the effort to achieve—only to end in another block of time invested halfheartedly with appropriately corresponding results.

WHY?

Why do you enter into any activity with anything but a commitment to achieve your objective of that

activity—not a desire to achieve your objective, but a commitment?

212° is not only a message of action—it's a message of persistent and additional action—the continual application of heat (effort) to whatever task or activity you undertake in order to achieve not only the primary objective you seek, but to reap the exponential rewards that are possible by applying one extra degree of effort.

How many opportunities have you missed because you were not aware of the possibilities that would occur if you applied a small amount of effort beyond what you normally do?

People develop personal habits toward action and rarely attempt to develop them further and continually. Unless someone engages in frequent self-review or an external source (a friend, a book, a manager, a spouse, a parent, an article, etc.) brings something to one's attention, a person will continue throughout life making very small improvements, if any at all.

Now you're aware of "212°—The Extra Degree." No longer will you be able to do only what is required of you and only what is expected of you. Because with this awareness comes responsibility—to yourself and to others. And, again...

YOU ARE NOW AWARE.

The excitement can begin. Are you smiling yet?

You now have a target for everything you do…

212°

You may not always be able to turn up the heat and hit the boiling point, but that doesn't mean you shouldn't make the attempt. It's what you'd advise others to do, and it's what we should teach our children.

211° can serve a purpose, but 212° is the extra degree—the extra degree that will bring exponential results to you and those you touch throughout your days.

There are no real secrets to success. Success with anything, success in anything, has one fundamental aspect—effort. To achieve exponential results requires additional effort. Take your courses. Read your books. Listen to your tapes. But take action.

Take action with commitment. Then, when you're ready for exponential results, apply the extra effort. Sometimes you'll have immediate exponential results

and sometimes you'll realize the benefits of your extra effort much farther down the road. Regardless, in many cases, it may only be that one extra push that gets you ten times the results you were attempting to originally obtain. Pace your expectations and operate at your new target—212°. You will realize the benefits of this extra effort. One extra degree can change everything.

At 211°, water is hot.
At 212°, it boils.
And with boiling water comes steam.
AND STEAM CAN POWER A LOCOMOTIVE.

It's your life.
You are responsible for your results.
IT'S TIME TO TURN UP THE HEAT.

From this day forward, commit to operating at 212° in everything you do. Etch it into your thinking—into your being. Apply it to your actions. It guarantees to increase your results positively and, in so many cases, increase your results exponentially.

212°
THOUGHTS
& FACTS

Professional golf tournaments are comprised of four rounds (games) of eighteen holes played over a four-day period (seventy-two holes total). Each year there are four major tournaments—the U.S. Open, the British Open, the PGA Championship, and the Masters. The average margin of victory between 1990 and 2014 (twenty-five years) in ALL tournaments combined was less than three strokes—less than a one-stroke difference per day. From 2000 through 2004 (five years), the winner across all tournaments took home an average of 78 percent more in prize dollars than the second-place finisher (before endorsements and other earnings).

"INCHES MAKE THE CHAMPION."

—Vince Lombardi,
Hall of Fame football coach, 1913–1970

2.40

The average margin of victory in strokes at the **Masters** (1990–2014)

That's 0.60 strokes per day.

....

77%

Additional prize dollars on average for winning **first place** at the Masters

First-place prize dollars: $917,640

Second-place prize dollars: $518,757

Playoffs needed to crown a winner after seventy-two holes: **six** (that's 24 percent of the time)

2.64

Average margin of victory in strokes at the **U.S. Open** (1990–2014)

That's 0.66 strokes per day.

- -

87%

Additional prize dollars on average for winning **first place** at the U.S. Open

First-place prize dollars: Second-place prize dollars:

$891,600 $475,702

Playoffs needed to crown a winner after seventy-two holes: **five** (that's 20 percent of the time)

2.72

Average margin of victory in strokes at the **British Open** (1990–2014)

That's 0.68 strokes per day.

76%

Additional prize dollars on average for winning **first place** at the British Open

First-place prize dollars: $886,446

Second-place prize dollars: $502,534

Playoffs needed to crown a winner after seventy-two holes: **seven** (that's 28 percent of the time)

2.32

Average margin of victory in strokes at the **PGA Championship** (1990–2014)

That's 0.58 strokes per day.

73%

Additional prize dollars on average for winning **first place** at the PGA Championship

First-place prize dollars: $905,800

Second-place prize dollars: $522,426

Playoffs needed to crown a winner after seventy-two holes: **seven** (that's 28 percent of the time)

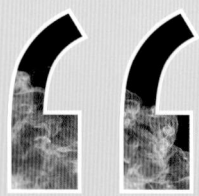

"TO GET WHAT WE'VE NEVER HAD WE MUST DO WHAT WE'VE NEVER DONE."
—Anonymous

"MANY OF LIFE'S FAILURES ARE MEN WHO DID NOT REALIZE HOW CLOSE THEY WERE TO SUCCESS WHEN THEY GAVE UP."
—Thomas Edison,
American inventor, 1847–1931

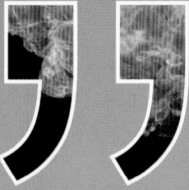

Horse racing's classic races include the Kentucky Derby, the Preakness, and the Belmont Stakes. A horse that wins each of these races in a single year is considered a Triple Crown winner—an unofficial title held by only twelve horses in the history of the sport. The Kentucky Derby and the Preakness last approximately two minutes, with the Belmont finishing at just over two and a half minutes. The average margin of victory between 2010–2014 (five years) over each of the Triple Crown races combined (fifteen races in all) was less than 1.5 lengths. Six races were won by less than a length (40 percent). The average payout to the winner over all fifteen races was 238 percent more than the horse that placed second.

> "COURAGE IS FEAR HOLDING ON
> FOR A MINUTE LONGER."
>
> —George S. Patton,
> American solider & general, 1885–1945

2.20

Average margin of victory in lengths at the Kentucky Derby (2010–2014)

....

256%

Additional prize dollars on average for winning first place at the Kentucky Derby

First-place prize dollars:
$1,425,840

Second-place prize dollars:
$400,000

0.95

Average margin of victory in lengths at the **Preakness** (2010–2014)

245%

Additional prize dollars on average for winning **first place** at the Preakness

First-place prize dollars: $760,000

Second-place prize dollars: $220,000

1.25

Average margin of victory in lengths at the **Belmont Stakes** (2010–2014)

196%

Additional prize dollars on average for winning **first place** at the Belmont Stakes

First-place prize dollars: $640,000

Second-place prize dollars: $216,000

"TRIUMPH OFTEN IS NEAREST WHEN DEFEAT SEEMS INESCAPABLE."

—B. C. Forbes,
founder & publisher of *Forbes* magazine, 1880–1954

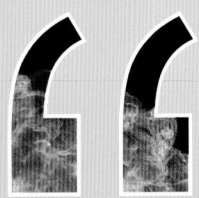

"THE LINE BETWEEN FAILURE AND SUCCESS IS SO FINE THAT WE... ARE OFTEN ON THE LINE AND DO NOT KNOW IT. HOW MANY A MAN HAS THROWN UP HIS HANDS AT A TIME WHEN A LITTLE MORE EFFORT, A LITTLE MORE PATIENCE WOULD HAVE ACHIEVED SUCCESS? A LITTLE MORE PERSISTENCE, A LITTLE MORE EFFORT, AND WHAT SEEMED HOPELESS FAILURE MAY TURN TO GLORIOUS SUCCESS."

—Elbert Hubbard,
American publisher & writer, 1856–1915

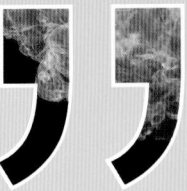

At 33°, water falling from the sky on a Saturday is a gray, rainy day.

At 32°, children are building snowmen, riding sleighs, and promising their parents that they're warm enough to stay outside five minutes longer.

A single degree can be the difference between gloom and a winter wonderland. Between a routine weekend and the magic of the season.

By making one extra mortgage payment a year, a thirty-year mortgage can be cut to twenty-two years.

A single degree can change everything.

Two of auto racing's premier events are the Daytona 500 (stock car) and the Indianapolis 500 (Indy car). Each takes three to three and a half hours to complete. In the fifteen-year period between 2000 and 2014, combining all thirty races, the winner took the checkered flag by an average margin of less than half a second (0.48) and took home $1,796,766 in first-place prize money. The average prize for the second-place finisher was $946,509—a difference of $850,257—a little more than half of the amount banked by the winner.

"YOU GIVE 100 PERCENT IN THE FIRST HALF OF THE GAME, AND IF THAT ISN'T ENOUGH, IN THE SECOND HALF YOU GIVE WHAT'S LEFT."

**—Yogi Berra,
Hall of Fame baseball player & manager, 1925–2015**

"NEVER STOP.
ONE ALWAYS STOPS AS SOON AS
SOMETHING IS ABOUT TO HAPPEN."

—Peter Brook,
British theater & film director, 1925–present

0.096

Average margin of victory in seconds at the **Daytona 500** (2000–2014)

45%

Additional prize dollars on average for winning **first place** at the Daytona 500

First-place prize dollars: $1,538,224

Second-place prize dollars: $1,062,217

0.87

Average margin of victory in seconds at the
Indianapolis 500 (2000–2014)

147%

Additional prize dollars on average for winning **first place** at the Indianapolis 500

First-place prize dollars: Second-place prize dollars:

$2,055,309 $830,801

212°
STORIES

212° SERVICE

Service is the lifeblood of any organization. Everything flows from it and is nourished by it. Customer service is not a department…it's an attitude.

Many companies talk the talk when it comes to customer service, but most fall short when it comes to delivering it on a consistent basis. One company that truly understands what 212° service is all about is the Ritz-Carlton Hotel Company. It's the only service company to twice capture the prestigious Malcolm Baldrige National Quality Award. Whenever possible, employees greet guests by name, they record details about guest preferences—from favorite drinks to

"YOU MAY HAVE TO FIGHT A BATTLE MORE THAN ONCE TO WIN IT."

—Margaret Thatcher,
British prime minister, 1925–2013

entertainment—and use the information to custom-tailor future stays. They also attempt to solve every problem they encounter, and any Ritz-Carlton employee can spend up to $2,000 to resolve a problem on the spot.

For the fifty-nine-hotel luxury chain, it starts with hiring positive, empathetic workers who are eager to please. Next comes twenty days of training before they even set foot in the hotel.

Once they start, however, every employee carries a small card with the company's twenty core values. What happens next separates Ritz-Carlton from the "Ritz-Carlton wannabes." Every day, all of the company's twenty-five thousand employees partake in a fifteen-minute session to discuss (and reinforce) one of those core values. What Ritz-Carlton has learned is that service doesn't just happen because of a prestigious name, but is delivered by reinforcing values and attitudes—on a daily basis! This, in their opinion, is the only way to ensure that values are transferred into actions and behaviors throughout the organization.

> "IN THE CONFRONTATION BETWEEN THE STREAM AND THE ROCK, THE STREAM ALWAYS WINS, NOT THROUGH STRENGTH BUT BY PERSEVERANCE."
>
> —H. Jackson Brown Jr., American author, 1940–present

212° ATTITUDE

The only thing that stands between a person and what he or she wants in life is the will to try it and the faith to believe it possible.

I've been an entrepreneur for over thirty years, and I've come to realize that the difference in success or failure is not how you look, how you dress, or how you're educated. It's how you think!

Early in my career, I was the vice president of sales for a food company. One time I was in Detroit hiring a salesperson for the market. We had lined up eight appointments for the day, and the morning had been a bust.

I looked up and my one o'clock appointment was standing at the door. He was a tall, good-looking guy, and I remember thinking, "This could be the one." We talked for about fifteen minutes, and I asked a question I always ask: "What will you be doing five years from now?" I'll never forget his answer. He said, "Mr. Anderson, the way these appointments have been going, I might still be interviewing!" Well, that wasn't exactly what I wanted to hear. We talked for a few more minutes and I excused him.

Then I looked up and my two o'clock was there—a short guy with a wrinkled sport coat. He walked over and gave me a confident handshake, and a few minutes later I asked the same question: "What will you be doing five years from now?" He looked me right in the eye and said, "Mr. Anderson, I'm going to be working for you. This job fits my skills and my needs to a tee. I don't just think, I know I can sell your product in this market. And furthermore, if you don't like my performance after thirty days, you don't owe me a cent."

Well, you could have knocked me over with a feather! He had just made me an offer I couldn't refuse. But the offer had nothing to do with the money I might save; it had everything to do with his unwavering passion and belief he could do it. Within a year, Bob was the number one salesperson in the company.

The power of a 212° attitude can be unstoppable.

"SOME MEN GIVE UP
THEIR DESIGNS WHEN THEY
HAVE ALMOST REACHED THE GOAL;
WHILE OTHERS, ON THE CONTRARY,
OBTAIN A VICTORY BY EXERTING,
AT THE LAST MOMENT,
MORE VIGOROUS EFFORTS
THAN EVER BEFORE."

—Herodotus,
Greek historian, c. 484–c. 425 BC

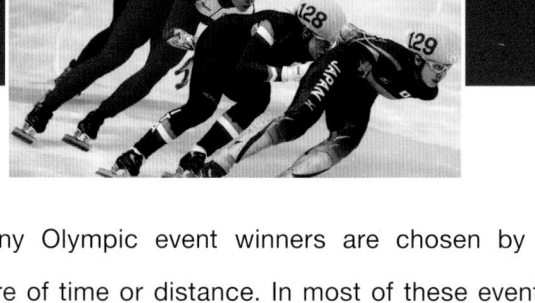

Many Olympic event winners are chosen by a measure of time or distance. In most of these events, the margin of victory between winning the **gold medal** and no medal at all is extremely small.

During the 2014 Winter Olympic games, the margin of victory between a **gold medal** and no medal at all was:

Men's slalom	**0.84 seconds**
Women's slalom	**0.82 seconds**
Men's four-man bobsleigh	**0.40 seconds**
Women's two-woman bobsleigh	**1.01 seconds**
Men's 500m speed skating	**0.32 seconds**
Women's 1000m speed skating	**0.28 seconds**

During the 2012 Summer Olympic games, the margin of victory between a **gold medal** and no medal at all was:

Men's 100m freestyle (swimming)	**0.29 seconds**
Women's 100m freestyle (swimming)	**0.45 seconds**
Men's 100m (running)	**0.17 seconds**
Women's 400m (running)	**0.18 seconds**
Men's long jump	**20 centimeters**
Women's marathon	**23 seconds**

212° LEADERSHIP

They don't care how much you know until they know how much you care.

On March 18, 2003, I turned on *Good Morning America* while eating breakfast. Charles Gibson was interviewing General Earl Hailston, the commanding general of Marine Forces Central Command. The general was waiting with his troops just a few miles off the border of Iraq—waiting to go to war. General Hailston is the only general in the armed forces who enlisted and came up through the ranks, and as he spoke, I was impressed by his humble and caring attitude.

Toward the end of the interview, his answer to a question touched me deeply. When Gibson asked him if he had any hobbies outside his work, the general said, "Yes, I love photography, especially taking photos of my men." He shared that while he had been waiting for the past few days, he would take photos of his men, and at night he would email the photos with a brief note to their mothers back in the United States. Gibson asked if he could see a sample of a letter, and the general walked into his tent and turned on his computer:

Dear Mrs. Johnson,

I thought you might enjoy seeing this picture of your son.

He is doing great. I also wanted you to know that you did a wonderful job of raising him. You must be very proud.

I can certainly tell you that I'm honored to serve with him in the U.S. Marines.

General Earl Hailston

Wow! I had goose bumps as I watched. I then watched Gibson interview a few of General Hailston's men. You could feel the genuine love and respect that they all had for their leader. You may have heard the quote, "They don't care how much you know until they know how much you care." Well, here's a man who truly understood what 212° leadership is all about.

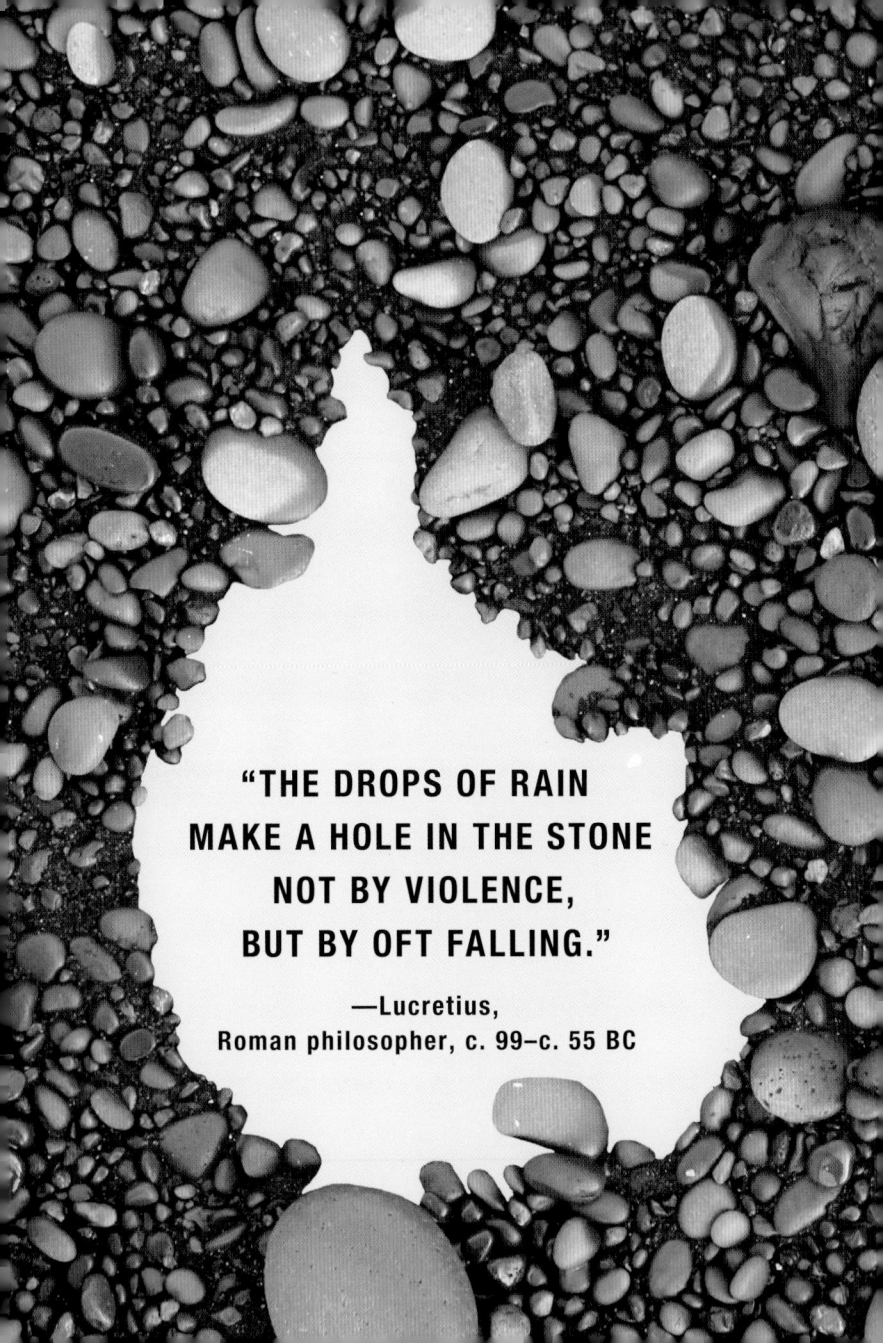

"THE DROPS OF RAIN
MAKE A HOLE IN THE STONE
NOT BY VIOLENCE,
BUT BY OFT FALLING."

—Lucretius,
Roman philosopher, c. 99–c. 55 BC

Oral Lee Brown receiving the Minerva Award in 2010.

212° KINDNESS

One of my favorite things to do is to wake up early on Sunday morning, get the Sunday paper, make a hot cup of coffee, and kick back to read about what's going on in the world. It's my quiet time, my time alone to reflect and relax.

One Sunday morning, about halfway through my little ritual, I spotted a headline that read "Graduating Student Credits His 'Angel.'" A young man who was graduating from college told the story about how Oral Lee Brown was his real-life angel. In 1987, Brown, a real estate agent in Northern California, saw a young girl in her neighborhood begging for money. When she went to the school the girl had claimed to attend, Brown couldn't find her, but that day she made a decision that would change the lives of many other children forever. She adopted an entire first-grade class in one of Oakland's lowest-performing schools, and she pledged that she would personally pay for anyone who wanted to attend college.

This would be a great story even if Oral Lee Brown were independently wealthy; however, it is a much greater story considering she was a former cotton picker from Mississippi, making $45,000 a year and raising two children of her own.

Brown lived up to her pledge. Since 1987, she's

personally saved $10,000 a year while also collecting donations for her "adopted first-grade kids." And because of her tremendous act of unselfish love, children who could have been "swallowed by the streets" are now graduating from college to pursue their dreams.

We all seek our purpose in life. Most of us wonder how we can make a positive difference during our brief time on this earth. But asking and doing are different things. Oral Lee Brown embodies what 212° kindness is all about.

"IT IS ONE OF THE MOST BEAUTIFUL COMPENSATIONS IN LIFE...WE CAN NEVER HELP ANOTHER WITHOUT HELPING OURSELVES."

**—Ralph Waldo Emerson,
American writer & poet, 1803–1882**

> "IF YOU WILL SPEND AN
> EXTRA HOUR EACH DAY OF
> STUDY IN YOUR CHOSEN FIELD,
> YOU WILL BE A NATIONAL
> EXPERT IN THAT FIELD
> IN FIVE YEARS OR LESS."
>
> —Earl Nightingale,
> American radio speaker, 1921–1989

212° COMMITMENT

Not too long ago, I had the opportunity to hear Jim Cathcart speak to a corporate audience. Jim is a good friend and a great speaker. He told the story of how listening to a radio program over twenty-five years ago changed his life forever, and with his permission I'd like to share it with you.

In 1972, Jim was working at the Little Rock, Arkansas Housing Authority, making $525 a month, with a new wife and baby at home, no college degree, no past successes, and not much hope for the foreseeable future.

One morning, he was sitting in his office listening to a radio program called "Our Changing World" by Earl Nightingale, who was known as the Dean of Personal Development. That day, Nightingale, in his booming voice, said something that would change Jim's life forever: "If you will spend an extra hour each day of study in your chosen field, you will be a national expert in that field in five years or less."

Jim was stunned, but the more he thought about it the more it made sense. Although he had never given a speech, he had always wanted to help people grow in areas of personal development motivation. He began his quest to put Nightingale's theory to the test by reading books and listening to tapes whenever he could. He also started exercising and joined a self-improvement study group. He persisted through weeks of temptations to quit, just by doing a little more each day to further his goal. Within six months he had learned more

than he had in his few years of college, and he began to believe he could turn his goal of becoming a motivational speaker into reality. All the hard work, the discipline, and study paid off. Jim now has delivered more than twenty-five hundred speeches worldwide and has won every major award in the speaking industry.

Just like companies have market value, so do people. In the simplest terms, your market value increases by knowing and doing more. You see, Jim really understood one of my favorite laws in life—you cannot get what you've never had unless you're willing to do what you've never done.

HE UNDERSTOOD THE POWER OF 212° COMMITMENT.

212° BELIEF

Belief fuels enthusiasm, and enthusiasm explodes into passion. It fires our souls and lifts our spirits. What happens when you believe something with all your heart?

In 1991, when Successories hired Tim Dumper as a corporate account manager, he shared his goal of becoming number one in the company with his manager, Neil Sexton. But Neil, quite frankly, had serious doubts that Tim could make it through the first month, much less be number one.

Neil's first two interviews with Tim were conducted over the phone, and he passed those with flying colors. But when Neil met Tim for the first time, he was shocked when Tim told him he was legally blind. He began to lose his sight when he was in the third grade from a rare disease called macular degeneration. Tim acknowledged he would have problems entering orders into the computer, but he had a possible solution. He told Neil about a machine that he could hook up to magnify the letters on the screen to two inches high. Tim was willing to buy it if he could have the job.

After the conversation, Neil came to my office and explained the situation. I said, "Neil, let's give him a chance." However, I must admit I had serious doubts that Tim could do it.

Well, we were dead wrong. We grossly underestimated Tim's passion and his determination to succeed. Even though it took him much longer to enter the orders, Tim made it work. He came in early. He worked late. Whatever it took, he did it.

In 1991, Tim's first year, he was number one out of ten experienced corporate sales reps, with over $500,000 in sales. In 1994, he was number one again with $700,000, and again in 1997 with $950,000. His customers loved him because when you can't see, you become a great listener. His peers loved him because of his caring, positive attitude.

He was certainly an inspiration to me too. I asked him one time, "Tim, how do you stay so positive?" He said, "Mac, it's unfortunate that I'm visually impaired, but I have to tell you that fighting through the adversity has made me a better person. I have come to realize that I have a lot more than I don't have. I love my family, my work, and the people I work with. I've been blessed in many ways."

Tim's 212° belief enabled him to overcome many obstacles and propelled him to success.

"WHETHER YOU THINK YOU CAN
OR THINK YOU CAN'T,
YOU'RE RIGHT."

—Henry Ford,
American business magnate, 1863–1947

212° FOCUS

212° focus is critical to your success in business and also in life. However, I must admit that this is something that took me a while to learn. "More is better" sounds reasonable, but I've learned the opposite is usually true. Less, I've discovered, is usually more. (This book is a good example.)

The reason, of course, is that there is something powerful about laser-like focus. Having simple, clearly defined goals can cut through the fog like a beacon in the night.

In 1981, Jan Carlzon had just been named the CEO of Scandinavian Airlines System. His company was in trouble. They had just been ranked by a consumer poll as the worst airline in the world. Last in service, last in dependability, and last in profits as a percentage of sales. Yet one year later, in the same poll, they were ranked number one in all three categories. What happened?

Carlzon had decided to focus on what he thought was the most critical issue: serving the customer. He wanted to keep it simple: identify every contact between the customer and the employee and treat that contact as a moment of truth. He set out to let his people know the importance of that moment, including the captain, the ticket agent, the baggage handler, and the flight attendant. "Every moment, every contact," he said, "must be as pleasant and as memorable as possible." He determined that he had approximately ten million customers each year, and on average each customer made contact with five of his people for approximately fifteen

Scandinavian Airlines (SAS) President Jan Carlzon
at event showing off SAS's new look; Kastrup
Airport, Copenhagen, Denmark (circa 1983).

seconds at a time. Carlzon felt that what happened in these fifty million contacts would determine the fate of his company.

He set out to share his vision with his twenty thousand employees. He knew the key was to empower the front line. Let them make the decisions and take action, because they were Scandinavian Airlines during those fifteen seconds. He now had twenty thousand people who were energized and ready to go because they focused on one very important thing: making every moment count. Carlzon made it happen with 212°.

"PERSEVERANCE IS NOT A LONG RACE; IT IS MANY SHORT RACES ONE AFTER THE OTHER."

—Rev. Walter Elliott,
American priest & missionary, 1842–1928

Image of rescue from Shackleton's failed expedition to the Antarctic (circa 1916).

212° PERSEVERANCE

Carl Mays, a speaker and author, recently shared an amazing story that I think captures the essence of 212° perseverance. I want to share it with you.

In December 1914, departing from South Georgia, an island in the Atlantic Ocean, Ernest Shackleton led a crew of twenty-seven men in a quest to cross Antarctica on foot, the last-known unclaimed prize in exploration annals. As they drew within eighty-five miles of the continent, their ship was trapped by unusually thick ice. Originally called *Polaris*, the ship had been renamed *Endurance* by Shackleton, a term derived from his family motto, *fortitudine vincimus*, which means "by endurance we conquer." This name proved to be prophetic.

Frozen fast for ten months, the trapped ship was eventually crushed and destroyed by the increasing pressure. Forced to abandon the ship, the men salvaged their lifeboats, camped on the ice for five months, and hiked to navigable waters. Amazingly, Shackleton and every crew member survived for twenty months in one of the most vicious regions of the world. They overcame extreme cold, breaking ice floes, leopard seal attacks, a shortage of food and drinking water, and finally two open boat trips.

The most remarkable of the small boat trips was a treacherous eight-hundred-mile ocean crossing back to South Georgia by Shackleton and a few of the men.

Endurance trapped in the Antarctic ice (circa 1916).

Today, that achievement is considered one of the greatest accomplishments in nautical history. After arriving at South Georgia, Shackleton led his team across the rugged, icy mountains, reached the island's remote whaling station, organized a rescue team, and went back for the others.

The miraculous outcome against horrendous odds was attributed to Shackleton's leadership. When interviewed later, every member of the crew said he highly respected and admired Shackleton throughout the entire two-year ordeal. Shackleton never doubted they would survive, and he communicated this confidence to the others. But his optimism was mixed with realism.

When it became clear the *Endurance* could not withstand the pressure of the ice, he made plans to abandon ship, set up camp, and search for additional possibilities. When they journeyed across the ice and Shackleton realized the need to discard weight, one of the first things to go was his valuable heirloom gold watch, which the men knew he greatly treasured. In the lifeboat journey through the frigid stormy sea, he daringly stood in the stern of the small craft and meticulously guided its course.

Shackleton maintained cohesion and cooperation among the men. He constantly emphasized, "We are one—we live or die together." He made it clear that he was in command, but he was always open to others' opinions and asked for input and suggestions. He led open discussions each evening and helped build social bonds among the men. He stressed courtesy and mutual respect. Everyone, including Shackleton, worked side-by-side and performed chores.

Shackleton defused anger. He wisely handled power struggles and dissidents before they could take hold, even sharing his tent with the potentially biggest dissenter. He had to alter short-term objectives and keep the men's energy on these objectives while never losing focus of the long-term goals. He found ways to lighten things up with humor and made sure there were always little successes to celebrate. His methods and actions eliminated what could have been devastating anxiety and despair among the men.

In the end, he knew that survival depended on a bold act, literally a do-or-die act, which was the attempt to reach an outpost by crossing eight hundred miles of tempestuous seas in an open boat. He took the chance. As a result, all twenty-eight men not only survived, but also became the epitome of the rewards that can come from belief, creativity, and 212° perseverance.

WHATEVER
IT
TAKES

212°
ACTIONS

Ideas for implementing the 212° mind-set in your life are suggested in the following pages. These are specific ways for you to begin taking 212° action right now—this week.

They're just the beginning for you. Grab hold of one or two and begin (or start with your own). Once you start, it'll be difficult for you to act in any other way. 212° will become a wonderful new habit in your world—a backdrop to all that you do—a habit that will create fantastic life results for you and help you serve as an influence to all those people around you.

REMEMBER...

WITH AWARENESS COMES RESPONSIBILITY... RESPONSIBILITY TO ACT.

AS A FRIEND

Choose to visit or talk with one extra friend each week and create fifty-two additional discussions among friends for the year.

Do something helpful and unexpected for one friend each week of the year and plant more than fifty additional possibilities of influence.

Forgive someone faster each week and put fifty-two better vibes out into the world every year.

Put your phone away once more each day when you're with someone. Add 365 more friendly and attentive moments to your year.

AS A PARENT

Wake and act each day with the understanding that your actions will be absorbed by your children, and your children will grow to be contributing adults to the level of your influence. Model one extra example each day and give your children 365 more moments of inspiration each year.

Add an extra fifteen minutes each day to the time you invest with your children—an equivalent of more than two weeks each year at work. Imagine the exponentially positive effect of investing two extra weeks each year exclusively in the development of your children.

AT WORK

Add a few hours a month to your professional development outside of the workday, knowing you'll have invested the equivalent of a full work week by the end of the year to your most valuable asset—you.

Make the extra contact each day: a sales call, a customer, a brief discussion with a colleague, an encouraging talk with a member of your team. With contact comes opportunity. At the end of the year you'll have opened more than two hundred additional doors of possibility.

AS A MANAGER

Act with the understanding that your management role has an objective of developing and encouraging others to succeed by doing the right tasks at the right time, every day, every week, and every month, to become the best they can possibly be. Share the 212° concept with them.

Apologize for and acknowledge one more of your mistakes each week—creating fifty more opportunities of trust and authenticity in your relationships each year.

Thank someone once more each business day and show your appreciation for others over two hundred more times each year.

IN A RELATIONSHIP

Invest a little money each year in blank greeting cards and mail one to your significant other or spouse each month (at home or at the office)—more than ten love notes each year are sure to create more than a few love moments.

Allow your partner to have the last word in two "discussions" each week where you'd normally dig your heels, and add not only one hundred events of kindness to your year, but probably an additional ten years to both of your lives.

If your loved one normally has charge of the children on a daily basis, take over the role one extra day each month and add almost two weeks a year to his or her personal time to recharge.

AS A STUDENT

Invest an extra hour of study each week in the course that most interests you, knowing that parts of it may become a piece of your life's work. At the end of the year, you'll have added the equivalent of one full workweek of dedicated study in your area of interest. This activity alone will put you far in front of the pack of those who do only what's required of them. This is what 212ers do.

Choose to focus without distraction on something (or someone) twice more each day and create more than seven hundred opportunities each year for better results.

IN YOUR COMMUNITY

Give a few extra hours each month to your cause, church, or group of choice. At the end of each year, you'll have added a full workweek to its goals and contributions.

Reflect twice more each month on who you know who might make a good addition to your cause or group (and who might benefit from being a part of it). Create the possibility for more than twenty positive connections each year.

AS A COACH

Plan your season and practices with the formal objective of developing the players' athletic and interpersonal skills in addition to having fun. Help them make the best use of their time.

Share the 212° message with your players and remind them, as examples present themselves, how the difference between scoring and not scoring (or defensively, stopping or not stopping a score) often comes down to a simple half step.

IN GENERAL

When you're working out, complete an additional repetition in your exercise because you know the big results are driven by the final repetitions, not the first.

Eliminate thirty minutes of television or web time each day and get back more than one hundred and eighty hours each year for something more important or fun (equivalent to four and a half weeks at work).

AND THEN SOME...

The secret to anyone's success is what I call "and-then-some" syndrome. The power of these words is captured in a poem written by Carl Holmes.

"And then some...these three little words are the secret to success. They are the difference between average people and top people in most companies. The top people always do what is expected...and then some. They are thoughtful of others; they are considerate and kind...and then some. They meet their responsibilities fairly and squarely...and then some. They are good friends and helpful neighbors...and then some. They can be counted on in an emergency...and then some. I am thankful for people like this, for they make the world a better place. Their spirit of service is summed up in these three little words...and then some."

212°
REFLECTIONS

PRACTICE KINDNESS

You see the opportunity. You are aware.

But you're busy.

"I need to be somewhere, doing something, otherwise I'd help."

"Someone else will do it."

"Someone else will pick it up."

"Someone else can handle it."

"It's not my responsibility."

212° THOUGHT

A person struggles. You help. A door needs to be opened. You open it. A piece of trash is in your path. You pick it up and throw it away. A child needs some extra attention. You give it. A job needs to be completed. You do it.

One more act of kindness a week will add fifty-two moments of inspiration to your year. Push it to two a week and you add more than one hundred. Imagine the possibilities.

212° COMMITMENT

Indulge your good side once more each week. Start now.

CEASE TO COMPLAIN

The weather.

The traffic.

My boss.

My customer.

My mother.

My father.

My sister.

My brother.

I don't have enough... But I really need...

I can't... If only [he, she, they] would...

It's been a tough [day, week, month]...

It's [Monday, Tuesday, Wednesday, Thursday, Friday]...

212° APPROACH

Be. Move forward. Cease to complain.

Your words move others. Your words move you. Make yours send everyone in the right direction.

Complaining once less a day chokes off 365 seeds of negativity a year.

212° COMMITMENT

Put a smile in the path of a complaint...once daily. Cease to complain.

PAUSE AND REFLECT

You skim the material.

"Great stuff."

"Really makes sense."

"I like that a lot."

You move on.

Quickly.

today
was a
good day

212° APPROACH

You read the material. You pause. You reflect. You give it thought. Deeper thought. You embrace it or toss it aside but you do so after pausing—after reflecting on it for more than an inattentive moment.

Thought is important because it is thought that generally precedes action.

Pausing and reflecting—investing thought beyond an instant twice more each week on a particular topic creates more than one hundred additional possibilities of action and/or improvement each year.

212° COMMITMENT

Pause and reflect—deeper—twice weekly.

PRUNE THE DIVERSIONS

When did you last evaluate the tasks you do every day against what's most important to you?

When did you last evaluate them against who's most important to you?

You have goals. You have time. You have energy.

Where should it be invested?

212° THOUGHT

Removing just two diversions from your life each week eliminates more than one hundred distractions a year from what's most important to you.

212° COMMITMENT

Prune the diversions. Twice weekly.

RISK. ATTEMPT.

Comfort. Risk.

Both are enjoyable.

One we strive to create. One we try to minimize.

One can make us lazy. One can make us stronger.

When did you last risk failure?

When did you last leave your comfort zone?

212° CHALLENGE

Step out of your comfort zone at least once each week and create over fifty additional opportunities for excitement, challenge, and possibility each year. This is what life's about.

212° COMMITMENT

Risk. Attempt. Fail. Succeed. Once more each week. It's been said that youth is wasted on the young.

By taking risks, we assure ourselves that life isn't wasted on the living.

ADD 10 MINUTES TO YOUR DAY

Alarm goes off. Snooze button is hit. The thought (if any at this hour): *Just ten more minutes.*

212° APPROACH

Night before. Alarm is set ten minutes earlier than usual. Next morning. Alarm goes off. The thought: *Beautiful. Ten more minutes I can add to my life.*

A small difference that adds the equivalent of over one and a half workweeks to your year to be used how you wish. What could you do with that extra time?

Push it to twenty minutes a day and you've just bought more time than most people get each year for vacation.

212° COMMITMENT

Add ten minutes to every day.

This is your wake-up call.

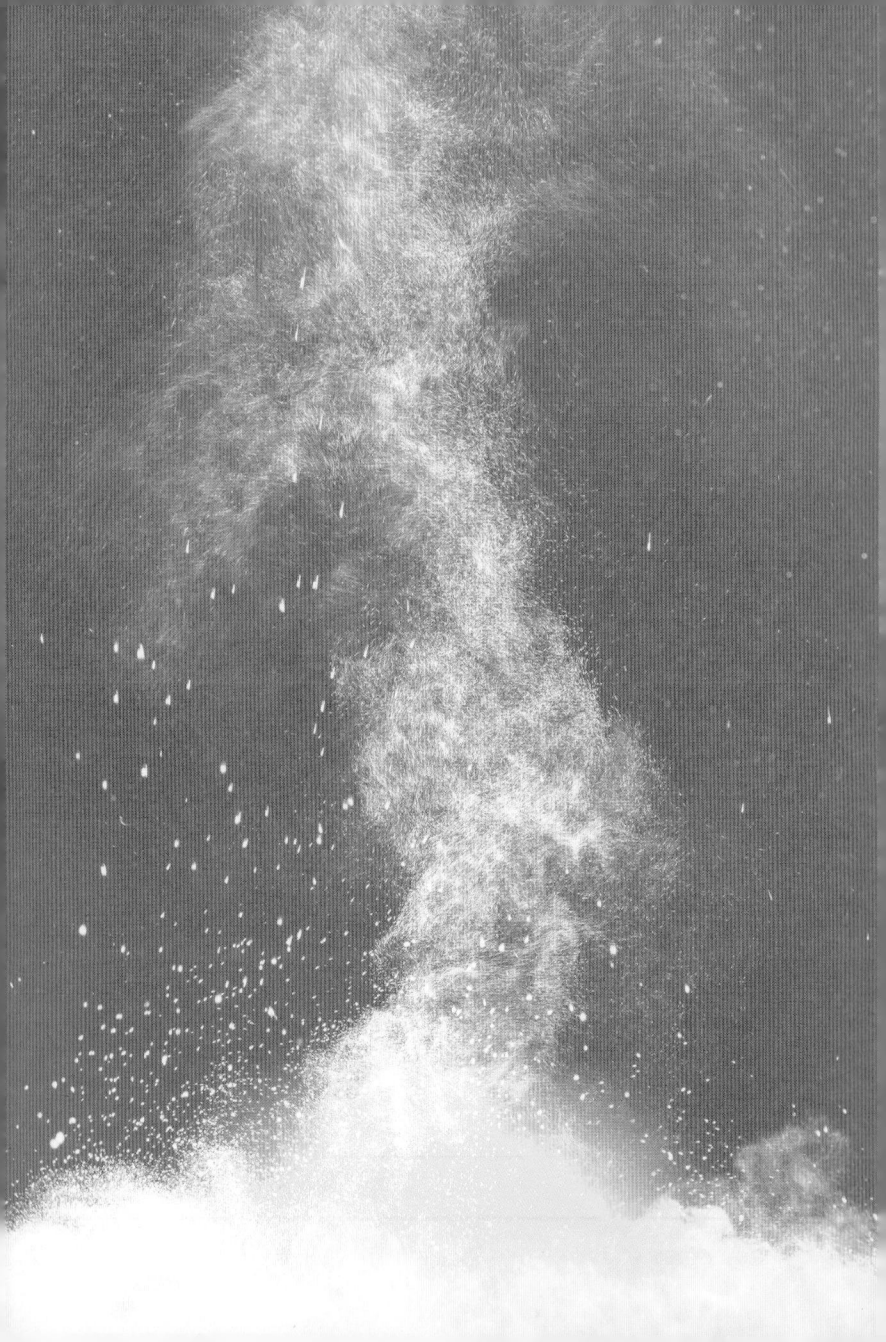

212°
AFTERWORD

Involvement and reminders drive continual awareness. And with awareness comes responsibility and action.

Let the number 212° serve as your constant reminder. It's your new way of thinking—your new way of acting. Write it down and leave it wherever it might serve you best—wherever you may need a prompt to extra action (or just action itself)—your bathroom mirror, the dashboard of your car, in your cubicle at work, on your refrigerator, above the door of your workout room.

**IT'S TIME TO
TURN UP THE HEAT!
GO TO WORK.**

ABOUT THE AUTHORS

SAM PARKER cofounded InspireYourPeople.com in 1998, which creates inspiring material to help people care more about their work and the people around them.

His other books include *Lead Simply*, *Smile & Move*, *Cross the Line*, and *Love Your People*.

Before InspireYourPeople.com, Sam sold products and services in several different industries.

A native of the Washington, DC, area, he now lives in Richmond, Virginia, with his wife (an artist) and their three children.

If you need a speaker for an event or you'd like to share feedback about 212, please email Sam at Sam@InspireYourPeople.com. If you're slightly more daring, call him at 804-762-4500 ext. 212.

MAC ANDERSON is the founder of Simple Truths (SimpleTruths.com) and Successories, Inc., the leader in designing and marketing products for motivation and recognition. These companies, however, are not the first success stories for Mac. He was also the founder and CEO of McCord Travel, the largest travel company in the Midwest, and part owner/VP of sales and marketing for Orval Kent Food Company, the country's largest manufacturer of prepared salads.

His accomplishments in these unrelated industries provide some insight into his passion and leadership skills. He brings the same passion in his speaking engagements to many corporate audiences on a variety of topics including leadership, motivation, and team building.

Mac has authored or coauthored seventeen books that have sold over three million copies. His titles include: *Change is Good … You Go First*, *Charging the Human Battery*, *Customer Love*, *Finding Joy*, *Learning to Dance in the Rain*, *212° Service*, *Motivational Quotes*,

The Nature of Success, *The Power of Attitude*, *The Power of Kindness*, *The Essence of Leadership*, *The Road to Happiness*, *The Dash*, *To a Child*, *Love is Spelled T-I-M-E*, *You Can't Send a Duck to Eagle School*, and *What's the Big Idea?*